CONTINENTS UNCOVERED

EUROPE

Written by Rob Colson
Illustrated by Josy Bloggs

Enslow PUBLISHING

Published in 2025 by Enslow Publishing, LLC
2544 Clinton Street
Buffalo, NY 14224

First published in Great Britain in 2023 by Hodder & Stoughton

Series Editor: Amy Pimperton
Series Designer: Ed Simkins
Illustrator: Josy Bloggs
Map illustrator: Amy Zhing

Manufactured in the United States of America

CPSIA compliance information: Batch #CSENS25: For further information contact Enslow Publishing LLC, New York, New York at 1-800-398-2504.

Please visit our website, www.enslowpublishing.com. For a free color catalog of all our high-quality books, call toll free 1-800-398-2504 or fax 1-877-980-4454.

Cataloging-in-Publication Data

Names: Colson, Rob, author. | Bloggs, Josy, illustrator.
Title: Europe / by Rob Colson, illustrated by Josy Bloggs.
Description: Buffalo, NY : Enslow Publishing, 2025. | Series: Continents uncovered | Includes glossary and index.
Identifiers: ISBN 9781978539136 (pbk.) | ISBN 9781978539143 (library bound) | ISBN 9781978539150 (ebook)
Subjects: LCSH: Europe--Juvenile literature.
Classification: LCC D1051.C657 2025 | DDC 940--dc23

We recommend adult supervision at all times while doing the activities in this book. Always be aware that craft materials may contain allergens, so check the packaging for allergens if there is a risk of an allergic reaction. Anyone with a known allergy must avoid these.

- Wear an apron and cover surfaces.
- Tie back long hair.
- Ask an adult for help with cutting and glueing.
- Check materials for allergens.

Find us on

CONTENTS

WHERE IN THE WORLD? 4

EASTERN EUROPE AND SCANDINAVIA 6

SOOMAA NATIONAL PARK 8

NORWEGIAN FJORDS 10

WESTERN AND CENTRAL EUROPE 12

ARDENNES 14

DARTMOOR 16

SOUTHERN EUROPE 18

CORSICAN SHRUBLAND 20

SWISS ALPS 22

PLITVICE LAKES 24

PEOPLE AND PLACES 26

QUIZ AND GLOSSARY 30

INDEX 32

WHERE IN THE WORLD?

Occupying the western side of the landmass of Eurasia, Europe is separated from Asia by the Ural Mountains. Europe sits entirely in the Northern Hemisphere and is the second-smallest of the seven continents. Most of Europe is densely populated, and it has fewer truly wild areas compared with other continents. It has extensive coastlines, with the Arctic Ocean to the north, the Atlantic Ocean to the west, and the Mediterranean, Black, and Caspian Seas along the south.

POLITICAL MAP

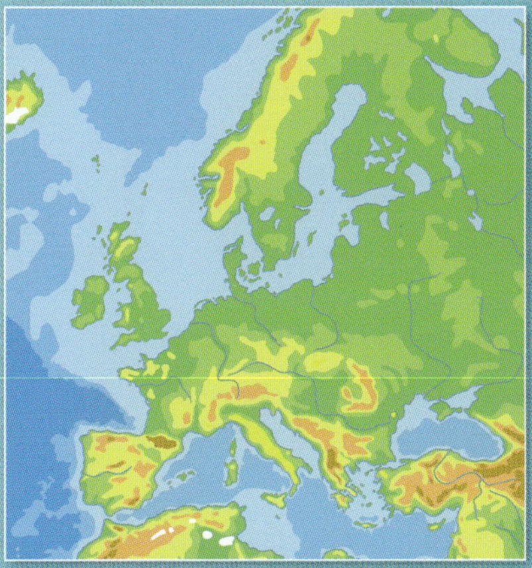

PHYSICAL MAP

MAKING MAPS

Mapmakers create maps that show different types of information. Political maps, such as the map of Europe at far left, show human features like countries. Physical maps use colors to show the geographical features of a region, such as altitude. For example, in the physical map of Europe (*left*), high ground is shown in brown and yellow, while low ground is shown in green.

HABITATS

A habitat is an area that is home to a particular group of plants and animals. The habitats of Europe range from the chilly Arctic north to the hot Mediterranean coast in the south. In the cold waters of the Norwegian fjords (1), whales and dolphins join with seabirds to feed on the plentiful fish. The forests of the Ardennes (2) are home to a wide variety of mammals and birds, while only tough animals can survive in the dry Corsican scrublands (3). High in the Alps (4), animals need to be sure of their feet to climb the steep mountain slopes.

FACTS

- Area: 3.9 million square miles (10.2 million square kilometers)
- Major rivers: Volga, Danube, Rhine, Rhône, Dnieper, Don, Loire
- Highest peak: Mount Elbrus, Caucasus Mountains, 18,510 feet (5,642 meters)
- Major mountain ranges – Alps, Caucasus, Pyrenees, Carpathians, Apennines, Scandinavian Mountains

EASTERN EUROPE AND SCANDINAVIA

Eastern Europe experiences warm summers but very cold winters. The landscape here is dominated by forests and grasslands. The Caucasus Mountains, straddling the border between Europe and Asia, are the highest mountains in Europe. Farther north, the landmass of Scandinavia extends beyond the Arctic Circle, where the land is mostly untouched by people.

BIAŁOWIEŻA FOREST

The Białowieża Forest on the border between Poland and Belarus is one of the last remaining sections of the vast forest that once stretched across most of northern and central Europe. This undisturbed wild area is home to 900 free-living European bison. The largest oak trees in the forest have been standing for more than 400 years. The oldest oak of all, known as Patriarch, is thought to be 600 years old.

SCANDINAVIAN TUNDRA

In the far north of Europe, much of Scandinavia is covered in a cold Arctic habitat called tundra. Low-lying plants, such as grasses, sedges, and lichens, dominate the landscape. A few inches below the surface, the soil is permanently frozen, which prevents trees from growing. The nomadic Sami people follow their herds of reindeer across the Scandinavian tundra, which is home to animals adapted to the cold, such as the lemming, the arctic fox, and the snowy owl.

EURASIAN STEPPE

The Eurasian Steppe is a huge area of grassland and shrubland that extends from central Europe into Asia. Much of the steppe has been converted to farmland, but the Tarutino Steppe in Ukraine is being returned to the wild. Animals, such as the kulan (wild ass), have been reintroduced to graze in the area. This will encourage the return of a wide variety of flowering plants, providing a diverse habitat for many more animals.

SOOMAA NATIONAL PARK

Soomaa National Park is a remote wetland area in Estonia. During winter, the wetlands freeze over, then each spring the area is flooded. Soomaa means "land of bogs" in Estonian, and it is Europe's largest continuous area of bogland. Many species of birds visit the wetlands each autumn during their annual migrations.

FACTS

- Estonia is home to Europe's largest population of Eurasian lynx. This secretive cat hunts mostly at night, searching for prey like rodents, deer, and other mammals.

- Water-loving beavers thrive in Soomaa. The beavers build dams across the park's waterways to create pools of deep water in which they build their homes, known as lodges.

THE "FIFTH SEASON"

Just 70 people live within Soomaa National Park. Each year, they must contend with a period of flooding known as the "fifth season." The melting of the snow at the end of winter transforms this low-lying basin into a lake up to 16 feet (5 m) deep. The residents' homes may be flooded for a whole month, during which time they move around the park by canoe.

ACTIVITY

Testing snowshoes

Winter hikers in Soomaa National Park cross the frozen land wearing snowshoes. See how snowshoes stop you from sinking in snow with this experiment using flour and a toy animal.

1. With an adult's help, fill a shallow pan with a few inches of flour. Do not pack the flour down. This will be your "snow."

2. Take a toy animal with four legs, such as a cat, and gently place it on the flour. How deep do its paws sink?

3. Now, with an adult's help, cut out four circles of cardboard that are several times larger than the toy's paws. These will be its snowshoes. Tape the circles to the paws and place the toy on the flour. The snowshoes spread the weight of the toy over a much larger area, so it should hardly sink at all. For this reason, the Eurasian lynx has very wide paws.

NORWEGIAN FJORDS

More than 1,000 fjords line the coast of Norway. These deep, narrow inlets of salt water are lined with mountains and towering cliffs. The longest fjord, Sognefjord, stretches 127 miles (205 km) inland and is more than 3,280 feet (1,000 m) deep. Large animals from the oceans, such as whales and sharks, are frequent visitors to the fjords.

FACTS

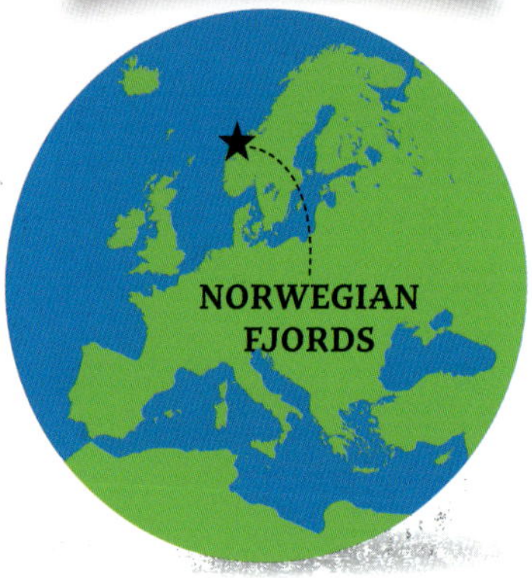

- Orcas, or killer whales, come to the fjords to catch herring. The whales work as a team to round up the fish in a technique known as "carousel feeding."

- In the breeding season, Atlantic puffins make their nests on the cliffs surrounding the fjords. The birds spend the rest of the year far out over the ocean.

MELTING GLACIERS

The fjords were formed by glaciers during ice ages over the last 2 million years. These sliding rivers of ice carved out deep U-shaped valleys on their way down to the ocean. As Earth emerged from ice ages, the glaciers melted, sea levels rose, and water flooded into the valleys.

ACTIVITY

Erosion in action

Norway's fjords were formed by erosion, with surface rock and soil worn down by glaciers. Watch the effects of erosion by water and ice with this simple experiment.

1. Ask an adult to help you pile soil on one side of a container, such as a shoebox, to create a slope. (Be sure to wash your hands after handling soil.)

2. Slowly pour water on to the top of the slope. Watch how it forms channels as it flows down the hill, pushing soil out of the way.

3. Now place ice cubes at the top of the slope and gently push them down the hill. How much soil do you move in the process?

LOUGH NEAGH

Lough Neagh is the largest lake on the island of Ireland. Water drains into the lake from the surrounding basin then empties into the sea via the River Bann. Lough Neagh is home to a large population of European eels. These snake-like fish start their lives 3,728 miles (6,000 km) to the west in the Sargasso Sea. From there, they cross the Atlantic Ocean and swim up the River Bann. They spend around 10 to 15 years in the lough before returning to the Sargasso Sea to spawn.

WESTERN AND CENTRAL EUROPE

The Alps mountain range dominates the center of Europe. To the west, the climate is affected by the Gulf Stream, a warm current in the Atlantic Ocean that brings mild winters. Rainfall is common throughout the year on the islands of Great Britain and Ireland, which is nicknamed the "Emerald Isle" because of its green landscape.

RHINE RIVER

The Rhine River rises in the Swiss Alps and flows north through Germany and the Netherlands to empty into the North Sea. In the Netherlands, the Rhine joins with the Meuse and Scheldt Rivers to create a wide delta made up of many different waterways. The Rhine passes through heavily industrialized areas and suffers greatly from pollution. In recent years, governments have made an effort to clean the water, and fish like salmon have returned to the river.

MASSIF CENTRAL

The Massif Central is a large highland region in southern France consisting of mountains and plateaus. Dense forests cover much of the area, giving way to rugged grasslands on the higher land that are grazed by cattle and sheep. On the southern fringe of the Massif Central is the remote Grand Causses, a limestone plateau cut through by narrow gorges lined with spectacular rock formations.

ARDENNES

The rolling hills of the Ardennes are covered by mixed forests of conifers and broadleaf trees. Rivers wind their way through the hills, cutting steep-sided valleys and creating spectacular cliff faces. The forests are home to a huge range of insects, mammals, and birds.

FACTS

- Red deer are the largest deer in the Ardennes. The male stags have huge antlers that can grow up to 3 feet (1 m) long.

- Ground-dwelling pheasants are common throughout the forests. The females are a plain brown color, but the males have brightly colored, shiny feathers.

WILD BOAR

Wild boar are found in many forests across Europe, and they thrive among the oak and beech trees of the Ardennes. They are large, powerful animals, capable of digging through frozen ground in search of food. Wild boar use their large snouts to sniff out food in the ground, a behavior known as rooting. They eat a wide range of plants and animals, but their favorite foods are nutrient-rich acorns and beechnuts.

ACTIVITY

Rainbow paper

As it moves around, the male pheasant's shiny coat appears to change color. This is called iridescence. Make rainbow paper to see iridescence in action.

1. Ask an adult to add one drop of clear nail polish to a bowl of water. The drop will spread across the surface.

2. Rest a piece of black construction paper on top of the layer of nail polish. Set the paper on a paper towel and leave it for a few minutes until it is dry.

3. Once the paper is dry, hold it up to the light. Tilt the paper at different angles and watch how the colors of the rainbow shimmer across it.

DARTMOOR

Dartmoor is an upland region in southwest England. It contains large areas of heath — open land with low-growing shrubs and grasses. The dramatic landscape is dotted with rocky hilltops known as tors. The climate is wet all year round, and in places water collects to create bogs formed of peat — the partially decayed remains of plants.

FACTS

- Every summer, marsh fritillary butterflies appear on the moor. These colorful insects lay their eggs on the devil's bit scabious plant. The caterpillars feed on the plants through the winter to emerge as butterflies the following summer.

- Polecats like the wet habitat of the moor. They hunt a range of prey, from mice and voles to small birds. The polecat is the ancestor of the domestic ferret.

DARTMOOR PONIES

Herds of free-roaming ponies range across Dartmoor. These hardy, sure-footed animals are well-suited to the harsh moorland weather, and their grazing helps to maintain plant life. Every autumn, the ponies are rounded up for the annual "drift," at which foals born in the spring are chosen to be sold. With their strong bodies and calm behavior, Dartmoor ponies are highly prized all over the world.

ACTIVITY

Squish painting

Create symmetrical colored butterfly wings with this squish painting.

1. On a sheet of white paper, drop a pattern of blobs of acrylic paint on one half of the paper.

2. Fold the paper in half with the paint inside. Use a craft stick to rub the paper and squish the paint around.

3. While the paper is folded, use scissors to cut out the shape of one butterfly wing. Unfold the paper to reveal your colorful butterfly! Ask an adult to help when using scissors.

PYRENEES

The Pyrenees Mountains extend for 250 miles (400 km) along the border between Spain and France. The highest peaks are more than 9,842 feet (3,000 m) high. A huge range of flowering plants grow on the foothills of the snowy peaks, including orchids and gentians. Many species of birds of prey, such as red kites, kestrels, and eagles, hover in the skies, looking for small mammals to eat.

SOUTHERN EUROPE

The land of southern Europe around the Mediterranean Sea experiences hot, dry summers and mild, wet winters. Much of the landscape is arid scrubland, which is turned brown by the summer sun. The summers are particularly hot in Greece in the eastern Mediterranean, where temperatures regularly soar above 95°F (35°C).

ITALIAN LAKES

In northern Italy, a series of long, thin, deep lakes are found in the foothills of the Alps. The lakes formed in valleys left behind when glaciers melted at the end of the last Ice Age. The region enjoys a warm climate with lots of sunshine, making it a popular destination for tourists. Many subtropical plants flourish on the shores of the lakes, which are famed for their colorful flower gardens.

MEDITERRANEAN SEA

With Europe to the north and Africa to the south, the Mediterranean Sea is almost entirely surrounded by land. In the west, it is connected to the Atlantic Ocean by the 8-mile- (13-km) wide Strait of Gibraltar. In the East, it is connected to the Black Sea by the 2,300-foot-wide (700 m) Bosphorus Strait. Protected from strong ocean currents, the Mediterranean provides a stable habitat for more than 17,000 species, most of which are found in the shallow waters of coastal areas.

CORSICAN SHRUBLAND

The island of Corsica in the Mediterranean Sea is covered in dense, low-lying plants in a habitat known as maquis shrubland. In the hot, dry climate, the largest plants are woody shrubs that grow a few yards in height. Some of Corsica's shrubs are found nowhere else in the world. Wildfires are commonplace, and many of the shrubs have special adaptations that allow them to survive the blazes.

FACTS

- The arbutus tree is one of the largest shrubs on Corsica, growing up to 50 feet (15 m) high. Each autumn, it produces white bell-shaped flowers, which turn into edible red berries.

- The mouflon is a species of wild sheep with large, curved horns. Originally found only on Corsica and neighboring Sardinia, the mouflon has been introduced to areas of mainland Europe.

CORSICAN DONKEY

Donkeys have lived on Corsica for at least 2,000 years. These domestic animals were used for transport and farming up to the 1960s, when there were more than 20,000 donkeys on the island. Today, only about 1,000 donkeys remain. These sure-footed animals are perfect companions on treks through remote, rocky areas of shrubland.

ACTIVITY

Coloring a leaf

Water travels up from the roots to the leaves of plants, such as shrubs. Watch how water moves through leaves with this simple experiment.

1. With adult help, find a large green leaf with a stem. Snip off the bottom of the stem with the help of an adult and place it in a glass about one-third filled with water. Add a few drops of red food coloring to the water so that you can see it travel through the leaf.

2. Place the leaf in a safe place and check on it each day for the next three days. Do you see the red color spreading through the leaf?

SWISS ALPS

Stretching over eight countries, the Alps are the highest mountain range entirely within the continent of Europe. The Alps cover about two-thirds of the area of the landlocked country of Switzerland. The rocky snow-capped peaks tower over green U-shaped valleys with grasslands and evergreen forests.

FACTS

- Growing at elevations of up to 9,850 feet (3,000 m), the edelweiss plant blooms between July and September, producing white star-shaped flowers that have become a symbol of the Alps.

- The alpine salamander is a small lizard-like amphibian. Most salamanders lay eggs, but the alpine salamander gives birth to live young, which spend up to three years growing inside their mother's body.

CHAMOIS

The chamois is a hardy mountain goat that lives in alpine meadows above the treeline during the summer, before moving down into the forests during the winter. Chamois are excellent runners and can jump more than 20 feet (6 m). When they feel threatened, they head for the highest ground they can find in the hope that any predator will find it difficult to match their amazing climbing abilities.

ACTIVITY

Edelweiss flower

Make a beautiful flower from colored construction paper.

1. With the help of an adult, cut a jagged mountain shape from a light blue piece of paper and glue it to a dark blue piece of paper.

2. Glue a green stem to the scene.

3. Arrange five large white petals in a ring at the end of the stem. Add five small petals between the large ones.

4. To finish your flower, add one large yellow circle to the center and arrange five smaller circles around it.

PLITVICE LAKES

Plitvice National Park is a mountainous region in Croatia with interlocking lakes that cascade into one another through a series of spectacular waterfalls. The area is formed of limestone rocks, which have eroded to create an extensive system of caves. Mixed forests of beech and fir trees cover the hillsides around the lakes, providing a mix of habitats for a wide range of wildlife.

FACTS

- Plitvice is one of the few areas in Europe where wolves are found. Three packs of wolves live there, hunting deer and other large mammals.

- More than 300 species of butterflies live around the lakes, including three rare blue species: the swamp blue, the large blue, and the mountain blue.

BATS

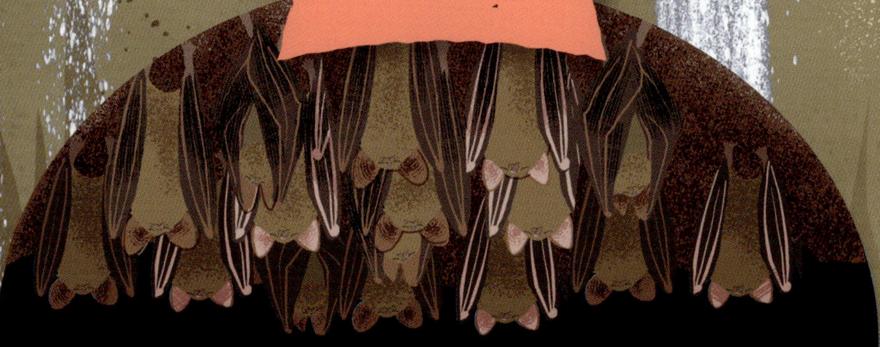

Twenty-two species of bats make their home in Plitvice National Park, including the rare long-fingered bat. During the day, the bats roost in caves in groups of up to 500 individuals. They come out at night to feed, hunting fish and aquatic insects over the lakes, rivers, and streams. The bats locate their prey in the dark using echolocation, giving off high-pitched sounds and listening out for the echoes bouncing back from objects around them.

ACTIVITY

Bat wings

A bat's wings are stretched around their long fingers. Calculate how far your fingers would need to grow to be bat-sized. What would your wingspan be?

1. With the help of a friend, use a tape measure to measure your body length from the bottom of your spine to the top of your head. Multiply this number by 2.5 to give the length of each wing.

2. Measuring from the center, place sticky notes on a wall at the place where your wingtips would be.

3. Stand in the center and stretch out your arms. How much longer are your bat wings?

UNITED KINGDOM

The United Kingdom (UK) occupies the island of Great Britain, part of the island of Ireland, and thousands of surrounding islands. It is made up of four countries: England, Scotland, Wales, and Northern Ireland. The country has a multi-ethnic population, reflecting its history as a world colonial power. Since the 1960s, the UK has been renowned for producing innovative rock and pop music, blending the cultural influences of its diverse population. The capital, London, is the most-visited city in Europe.

UNITED KINGDOM

AREA: 93,823 SQUARE MILES (243,000 SQ KM)

POPULATION: 68 MILLION

MAIN LANGUAGE: ENGLISH

CAPITAL CITY: LONDON

PEOPLE AND PLACES

Europe has a population of 750 million people spread over more than 40 different countries. Northern Europe is the wealthiest part of the continent, and the people of Scandinavia in the far north enjoy a very high standard of living. The various countries are well-connected by road and train networks, and people often move from country to country to find work.

THE EU

The European Union (EU) is a political organization of 27 European countries that share a common market and allow their people to move freely across country borders. The population living in the EU is 450 million, which is about two-thirds of the total population of the continent. In addition to their national governments, citizens of the EU also elect a European Parliament, while the Court of Justice of the European Union oversees the application of laws voted on by the parliament.

PARIS

The capital city of France is one of the most popular tourist destinations in the world. Attractions include the Louvre, the world's second-largest art museum. The Catacombs are an unusual attraction. This maze of tunnels 65 feet (20 m) under the streets of central Paris houses the remains of more than 6 million people. The bones were moved there from the city's overflowing cemeteries more than 200 years ago. Half a million people visit the bone-lined tunnels each year.

SPAIN

Spain shares the Iberian Peninsula in southwest Europe with Portugal. The official language is Spanish, but in autonomous regions, such as Catalonia and the Basque Country, regional languages are widely spoken. Spain is famed for its lively festivals, including La Tomatina in the town of Buñol, an annual event during which thousands of people pelt one another with tomatoes!

SPAIN

AREA: 195,368 SQUARE MILES (506,000 SQ KM)

POPULATION: 47.4 MILLION

MAIN LANGUAGE: SPANISH

CAPITAL CITY: MADRID

PEOPLE AND PLACES

In southern Europe, a series of countries line the northern coast of the Mediterranean Sea, from Turkey in the east to Spain in the west. The Balkans in southeast Europe is a region with a varied mix of cultures and religions, reflecting a history during which the area was invaded from the east and the west. Millions of people from northern Europe spend their holidays in the south, enjoying the hot, dry summers and warm seas.

ITALY

Italy occupies a long peninsula that extends far into the Mediterranean Sea. The national language is Italian, but many dialects are spoken. The country has a number of historic cities, such as Florence and Venice, with art and architecture dating back to the Middle Ages. The capital, Rome, is also the home of Vatican City, a tiny city-state that is the headquarters of the Catholic Church and houses many famous artworks, including the ceiling of the Sistine Chapel, painted by the artist Michelangelo.

ISTANBUL

The Turkish city of Istanbul straddles the Bosphorus Strait, which marks a boundary between Europe and Asia. With a population of 15 million, Istanbul is the largest city in Europe but isn't the capital of Turkey. Ankara, farther east, is Turkey's capital city. On the European side of the Bosphorus sits the Hagia Sophia. This was built in the 6th century CE as a Christian church during a time when the city was known as Constantinople. It was converted into a mosque in the 16th century, when the city became part of the Ottoman Empire and changed its name to Istanbul.

QUIZ

1. What is the highest mountain in Europe?
2. The Tarutino Steppe is located in which country in eastern Europe?
3. What is the name of the home beavers build for themselves in pools of deep water?

4. What is the name of the nomadic people who herd reindeer across the Scandinavian tundra?
5. The Strait of Gibraltar connects the Atlantic Ocean to which sea?
6. Where do the eels that live in Lough Neagh start their lives?
7. How many species of bats make their home in Plitvice National Park?
8. Which mountain range extends for 250 miles (400 km) along the border between France and Spain?
9. The mouflon was originally only found on Corsica and which other island in the Mediterranean Sea?
10. Name the four countries that make up the United Kingdom.
11. Which tiny city-state is located entirely within the city of Rome?

12. The Hagia Sofia is a building in which city that straddles the Bosphorus Strait?

Answers:
1. Mount Elbrus **2.** Ukraine **3.** lodge **4.** the Sami **5.** Mediterranean Sea **6.** the Sargasso Sea **7.** 22 **8.** the Pyrenees Mountains **9.** Sardinia **10.** England, Scotland, Wales, and Northern Ireland **11.** Vatican City **12.** Istanbul

GLOSSARY

Alpine
Relating to mountains, especially the Alps.

Amphibians
A group of animals, including frogs, that can live both on land and in water.

Arctic Circle
A line of latitude in the Northern Hemisphere at approximately 66° North.

Bogland
An area of wetland in which dead plant material called peat accumulates.

Climate
The weather conditions in a region averaged over a long period of time.

Delta
A triangular shaped region formed when a river spreads out before entering the sea.

Dialect
A regional form of a language that features its own vocabulary and rules of grammar.

Domestic
Relating to animals that are bred to live with people.

Evergreen
A type of plant that keeps its leaves all year.

Habitat
An area with the right conditions for a particular set of living things.

Ice age
A period when temperatures were lower and large ice sheets covered much of the surface.

Limestone
A form of rock that is dissolved by water.

Lough
An Irish word for a lake.

Middle Ages
A period in European history from the end of the Roman Empire, around 476 CE, to about 1500.

Migration
The movement of animals from one place to another.

Ottoman Empire
An empire that stretched through Turkey into Europe, Africa, and Asia and lasted from about 1300 until the First World War (1914–18).

Peninsula
A thin strip of land that sticks out into water.

Plateau
(Plural: plateaus) An area of high, flat ground.

Predator
An animal that hunts and eats other animals.

Scrubland
An area in which low-lying trees and shrubs grow.

Shrubs
Small or medium-sized woody plants.

Species
A group of closely related living things that reproduce with one another.

INDEX

Alps 5, 12, 22–23
Arctic Circle 6
Ardennes 5, 14–15
area of Europe 5

Balkans 28
bats 24, 25
beavers 8
Białowieża Forest 6
bison 6
bogland 8, 16
Bosphorus Strait 19, 29
butterflies 16, 24

Caucasus Mountains 6
chamois 23
climates 6, 12, 16, 18
coastlines 4
Corsica 5, 20–21
Croatia 24–25

Dartmoor 16–17
deer 7, 14
donkeys 20

eastern Europe 6–9
eels 12
England 16–17
Estonia 8–9
Eurasian Steppe 7
European Union (EU) 27

fjords 5, 10–11
forests 6
France 5, 13, 14–15, 18, 27

glaciers 11, 19
Grand Causses 13
Great Britain 12, 16–17, 26
Greece 18
Gulf Stream 12

habitats 5
Hagia Sofia 29

Iberian Peninsula 28
Ireland 12, 26
Istanbul 29
Italy 19, 29

kulan 7

location of Europe 4
Lough Neagh 12
lynx 8

maps, political and physical 5
maquis 20–21
Massif Central 13
Mediterranean Sea 19
mouflon 20
mountains 5, 6, 12, 18, 22–23

Netherlands 13
Norway 5, 10–11

orcas (killer whales) 10

Paris 27
pheasants 14
Plitvice National Park 24–25
polecats 16
ponies 17
population 26, 27
puffins 10
Pyrenees 18

Rhine River 13
rivers and lakes 5, 12, 13, 19, 24–25

salamanders 22
Sami people 7
Scandinavia 6, 7, 10–11, 26
shrubland 7, 20–21
Soomaa National Park 8–9
southern Europe 18–25, 28–29
Spain 18, 28
Strait of Gibraltar 19
Switzerland 22–23

Tarutino Steppe 7
tundra 7
Turkey 29

Ukraine 7
United Kingdom 26

Vatican City 29

western and central Europe 12–17
wild boar 15
wolves 24